NICE AND LOUD

NICE AND LOUD

Poems by Lois Rosen

TEBOT BACH • HUNTINGTON BEACH • CALIFORNIA • 2015

Nice and Loud

©2015 Lois Rosen

Book design: Michael Wada
Cover Art: Susan Trueblood Stuart
Author Photo: Susan Lee Graves

ISBN 10:   1-939678-16-1
ISBN 13:   978-1-939678-1-64

Library of Congress Control Number: 2015944579

A Tebot Bach book
Tebot Bach, Welsh for little teapot, is a Nonprofit Public Benefit Corporation, which sponsors workshops, forums, lectures, and publications. Tebot Bach books are distributed by Small Press Distribution, Armadillo and Ingram.

The Tebot Bach Mission: Advancing literacy, strengthening community, and transforming life experiences with the power of poetry through readings, workshops, and publications.

This book is made possible through a grant from The San Diego Foundation Steven R. and Lera B. Smith Fund at the recommendation of Lera Smith.

www.tebotbach.org

OTHER TITLES BY LOIS ROSEN

POEMS

Pigeons

FICTION

Chapbook

Layer Cake

Acknowledgments

Grateful acknowledgment is made to the following publications in which these poems, some in slightly different forms, first appeared:

Alimentum: The Literature of Food Nonpareil
CAB: Conversations Across Borders Cake and Bread, Lathyrus Maritimus: Beach Peas
Calapooya Collage A Life's Alphabet, Feeding the Pigeons, Goodwill Offering
Calyx Hide-a-Bed, The Only Land She Ever Owned Was Her Plot at Mt. Hope Cemetery, Provider, First Communion
Clackamas Literary Review Oy, Yonkers
Crab Creek Review Cordate Shape
Drash Moving Her
Fireweed *Adiós,* Roberto, Department of Labor Senior Investigator
Gold Man Review Peaches
Homestead Review Wonders Never Cease
Hubbub Praise
International Poetry Review The Sorrow of Meshari al Gharabali
Many Mountains Moving Harbor, *Cinco de Mayo*
On the Issues Cherries, Bananas, and a Little Black Veil
Oregon Writers Colonygram Pantoum for Dorothy at 92
Verseweavers My Building, Singer Arms
VoiceCatcher First Communion
Windfall Autumn Retreat on the Breitenbush River
Writers' Forum River We Are Warned Against Before We Ever Come Here

For

Kevin Davidson

NICE AND LOUD

Contents

I.

II.

III.

IV.

V.

I

CAKE AND BREAD

We didn't worry about weight then
so soon after the war. Uncle Benchie
arriving from somewhere, maybe Poland,
Russia – some Jew-killer country
not to be talked about with children
though I heard him mutter
Stalin bren un zeller: Yiddish
for "Stalin burn in hell."

And though our clothes
came from Klein's basement,
we gobbled seven-layer cakes,
chocolate cream pies,
charlotte russes,
linzer tortes
with raspberry jelly oozing.

We didn't need to worry
about hooligans, bloody
round-ups or pogroms.
Night after night, Papa
returned home unbeaten,
white boxes gleaming
from the bakery,
bags brimming with challah,
frozen-dough rolls, seeded rye.
He repeated, "Never
save on your stomach."

GROSBEAK

Apologize, mother, for my birth,
red and female:
squeeze until I fit
into grandfather's name
shortened by one vowel.

Force-feed me
until I gag.
Say I eat like a bird:
magpie, cuckoo, grosbeak.

Make me kiss Mrs. Kaminetsky,
thank her for her honey cake.
*Whining ungrateful child,
your face will freeze like that.*

If I wave at cars,
make me roll up the windows.
Point toward a policeman
ready to arrest me.

Mama, I won't stare at
Mr. Ruben's fingers made stubs
from cutting windows. I won't
scream when cockroaches
race toward me.

A blanket tucked in
can protect me. I will hide
behind Papa's armchair,
huddle under his prayer shawl,
white sail to catch the wind.

WHITE FEATHER

Yoo hoo, it's me.
My name is Pinky Lee.

the man in a red-checked jacket, baggy pants,
and gigantic pink tie
sings on our TV.

His blue and white checked cap's teensy.
Maybe he's bald, forgot his hat,
and grabbed a little boy's.

I lied about the colors.
Our TV's black and white,
but I did see pictures in *Life*.

When icky
Pinky Lee comes on,
I turn off the TV quick.

If I saw him on my side of Broadway,
I'd run across the street
even if traffic was coming.

But today I'm home sick on the couch,
twirling a white feather
from the cushion.

I saw the end sticking out and pulled.
It's big as my pinky.
Pinky Lee's a very silly name for a man.

Mama covers me with a blanket
and gives me a cup of Lipton's
with a teaspoon of grape jelly in it.

The jelly's like an island on the cup's bottom.
I wish Pinky Lee would go there
and never come back.

ARCADE

Oh Nettie dear, I'm loving you
And that's the way I feel, O Nettie dear,

my off-key father croons in the 42nd Street
penny arcade recording booth
around his made-up melodies
the predicted blizzard starting to rage.

In our ready-made igloo,
we two Eskimos survive
no matter what his doctors say
or don't say about months to live.

The needle engraves
his voice
into black vinyl.

Take that,
you arctic winds!
Take that,
you walruses with tusks!

We have all
the seal meat and blubber
we need to keep us both here
one hundred percent
alive.

AFTER THE WAR

Uncle David came home whole
to the house on Shelly Avenue
white siding, grass, the orange tang
of marigolds he planted,
no warning labels on packages
those days before filters.
A snowball bush bloomed spheres
dazzled by sun, and the sprinkler
made small rainbows. My uncle
and aunt watched us cousins splash
together in a wading pool, before
it mattered if we wore bathing suits.

He brought miniature porcelain
furniture made in Limoges
decorated with foreign purple flowers.
He'd fought in France where Lanvin
created *Arpege*, *Rumeur* and My Sin,
where Bartholdi and Eiffel
designed Liberty, the statue
our family watched for a nickel
from the Staten Island Ferry,
my father holding my hand
where the ocean smell, gulls,
and the view of Manhattan
belonged to us no matter
who we were

SCHNAPPS

No Yonkers beautician whacked off hair that way. Shorn,
that's how she looked, like a girl who'd been shaved bald
by the Gestapo and a month later some hair grew in.

But it wasn't Nazis, not in '57. We were born after the war—
though she in Hungary, pale Agnes Kronberger who spoke our
language with an accent. *Be polite. Include the nice girl*,
Mom insisted.

Did I ask Agnes one thing about Hungary?
Did I ask what she'd been through there?

She played jump rope, tossed her red ball and grabbed jacks
like the rest of us, but her bones stuck out.
Didn't she have enough food in America?

Her father got a job right away.
Men in our synagogue made sure of that.
The congregation's Sisterhood brought her mother to events.
She spoke Hungarian with Mrs.Geller, who'd escaped earlier
so Agnes and her family were not alone.

Play with us, I spat at her, as if I'd just sipped
their Hungarian brandy, the bottle of Schnapps
her family thanked us with, toasting *L'chaim, To Life,*
the liquor burning my unwilling tongue.

FEEDING THE PIGEONS

To the Bowery, Papa and I bring stacks
of stale bread. I hold my father's pale
hand tight. Pigeons peck at crumbs
we scatter. Sad men at the stoplight
wipe windshields with wet gray rags.
Old Lady Frankel wears Wonder Bread
sacks on her feet, stops in doorways to beg.

How can birds' hollow bones support them?
How do homing pigeons know the way?
Pigeons, squirrels, rats, the same gray squalor.
Papa and I on the green bench together.
Wind blows hair in my mouth when the birds
fly away, when I hear my voice calling
Pidgee, don't go pidgee.

DID YOU LIKE IT AT SUMMER CAMP?

After living with you, all three of us in this minuscule
apartment, ninety-degree heat, hundred-percent humidity,
no air conditioning, zero cross-ventilation,
Dad traipsing around in boxer shorts,
you in housedress and curlers,
me glued to *Father Knows Best*,
Our Miss Brooks, women coifed and gloved,
no fathers in undershirts, family pets with real fur,
lonely goldfish leaping from a bowl, choosing suicide
over life in that environment. Did I like it?

Badminton, volleyball, baseball, tennis, dancing,
morning swim lessons, afternoon free swims,
moonlight skinny dips, canoes to paddle alone,
no one to say, *You'll get hurt. You'll get dirty.*
Cook Anna Mae's tapioca, fresh blueberry pies,
no bar to my disappearing chubbiness,
licking sticky s'mores from my fingers.

A whole cabin full of girls: Pat Cantor, Eileen Ruzow,
Susan Lesh, my favorites of anyone. Kind girls, smart girls—
we sang the entire score of the *King and I* with a girl king,
singing loud as our lungs could fling every note
at bonfires higher than our heads, things you
would have forbidden.

I memorized every camp song
like I was born to them:
Each campfire lights anew-oo-oo
The flame of friendship true-oo-oo
our girl voices booming across the lake:
I don't wanna go home.
The buses they rumble.
The trolleys they roar.
I don't wanna go home anymore.

II

FIRST COMMUNION

Had I ever held a flower before?
Maybe a dandelion in a park.

After the O'Connors invited me
to their country house,
I returned home hugging
an armful of peonies.

No longer was I fourth-floor-walkup-
father-had-cancer-and-could-die-no-
room-of-her-own Lois Liebowitz.

Something lush
had been given to me.

Something about me had made
this family of Catholics offer flowers
though Daddy swore Johnny O'Connor
was *a real anti-Semite.*

I brought the bouquet
into our cramped apartment.

Blooms big as babies' heads
in a Dellwood Dairy milk bottle
graced our coffee table
beside Mama's ashtrays
of lipsticked Lucky Strike butts.

I'd brought home
something unJewish as lobster.
They smelled like perfume.

OUR DAILY BREAD

In our case,
daily bagel.
The list of *trespasses*
begins with birth,
a one-bedroom apartment
already too small,
a toddler upsetting *chachkes*,
teenage fists breaking
living room door panes.
My every word overheard,
"The Temptations" on the phonograph:
Shoo doop and shoo be doop,
screams to *turn that thing down.*
Deliver us, seltzer man
climbing flights of stairs,
case of bottles on your back.
The kingdom is Scarsdale:
big houses and lawns,
not this hallway where brown
aluminum closets hulk,
crammed so full you wonder
they don't explode. *Glory,*
is the magnificent seven-layer cake
from Yonkers Pastry
a triumph of engineering,
Eddie Cantor's voice
singing *"Kol Nidre"* so sweetly
a child could weep.
Forever is how long our family
will be stuck in
that fourth-floor walkup.

CHERRIES, BANANAS, AND A LITTLE BLACK VEIL

Men, men, men in their yarmulkes
and prayer shawls at the Sons of Israel
Barry Cohen's father called to the Torah
on the High Holy Days, a Kohan
from the *numero uno* tribe of the twelve.

Mom in a hat topped with cherries,
bananas, and a little black veil
in the second floor balcony
because God forbid, a pious man in prayer
would see her hair and, *Oy Gevalt,*
drop his *siddur*–his zipper, his pants.

Me, Grandma, and Mrs. Kushalevsky,
the sirens of Elliott Avenue,
Medusas, three deadliest
of The Seven Sins,
The Kosher Temptations
Do-ah, do-ah, girdled and gartered,
because gorgeous Delilah
seduced Samson as if he had no say,
as Eve tempted Adam,
Hey, bite this apple, Sweetie Pie.

Adam, practice this:
No, thank you. I'm just not hungry
Puh lease
Cover your eyes.
Pick some fig leaves.
Press them firmly to your eyelids.
Just don't dare say it's the woman's fault,
cover her up in a hat,
a snood,
a headscarf,
a burka.
Or better yet
try sitting in the synagogue balcony
on a ninety degree day in a girdle and stockings.
Don't you dare distract us for one second
while we women sway and sing.

PEONIES

Ants remove the paste
covering the bud.
Mother says, *Don't
let men lure you in cars,*
but I lie on the rug
your hand on my breast.

Peonies burst pink.
Hydrants spray rank sidewalks.
The snow cone man sings *papaya.*
Past a block of ruined buildings
Estella swings her bare legs.

Peonies don't hold back.
They open up fragrant
as puffs of French talcum
like the laughter of girls
waltzing on splinters.

HARBOR

Out of littered sidewalks and subways, into
centuries-old gardens of fern and begonia,
strawberries served on Royal Copenhagen.
How could I tell
Scovrider Due about the pinched
little berries packaged in plastic
at the A&P—or say I never had
my own bedroom, that cancer
turned my father miserly,
how I wore a green uniform
the color of worn-out dollar bills
bagging groceries at Daitch Shopwell,
saved the money, hid the application,
and the scholarship was a miracle.

In Denmark, of all countries in the world
a Jewish girl, on her own could be safe,
even if the story about King Christian
wearing a star of David to defy the Nazis
was a myth. Danes smuggled out
their Jews. There really were red roofs
with stork nests, cobblestone streets,
and a cottage in Odense where
Hans Christian Andersen composed
the dark, instructive tales Disney
turned into happily-ever-after.
If only *The Ugly Duckling*
was really a swan,
if only *The Little Mermaid*
could dance like this Yonkers girl who ran
bare-legged into the North Sea,
after a Danish boy named Jorgen
covered her face and neck with kisses.
But who was I kidding?
In Copenhagen Harbor, the naked mermaid
was fused to a rock

At Alexander's Department Store, I'd be jostling
for girdles heaped like flounder
on the bargain table, opening letters,
unable to answer the easiest question,
How are you? A prune danish,
a cheese danish—my life.
Mermaid with legs,
every step inland searing

PROVIDER

You will be well provided for, Father promised,
but Mother and I never suspected
twenty thousand cash in the file drawer.
Hundred-dollar bills, the wad held together
with dry rubber bands—cracking in our hands.

I figured I understood his reasons: early manhood
during the Depression, the Liebowitz real estate business
belly-up, dazed Jewish refugees sleeping in his parents'
living room. Escape needs bribes—even if the bank's open,
there might not be time for a withdrawal.

The cancer he had before I was born never recurred,
it could. The polio he suffered
had left one leg thin. Since he insisted
we three live in that sardine can apartment,
what could Mother and I say?

Why should Father go to doctors whose predictions
he'd outlived for twenty years?
How could any of us know the boils, the hunger
for sweets, and thirst were signs?
One night, he slipped into a diabetic coma,
the next day, he was dead.

After the funeral we found bank books, bonds,
those dollars we flipped through like cards,
screamed, clapped, giggled like hell,
our blouses soaked with tears.

GOODWILL OFFERING

I wore you once to a country club
none of us was rich enough to join.
Lilac chiffon, full skirt
undulating below my knees,
ruffled rows gathered at the waist,
bodice tucked close:
my prom dress

with a neckline never intended
for a chubby adolescent,
the plunging in back and front
and thin straps strained almost to breaking.

My apartment window chorus applauded
the princess, an ugly duckling
fooling no one.
I and the boy chafing in his tuxedo
danced far enough apart to avoid
pregnancy or locking eyeglasses.

So much for fanfare,
and the boy I tried to follow
who kept stepping on my feet.
On the hanger you made a promise
that exposed too much of me.

MY BUILDING, "SINGER ARMS"

Bessie Smith, Ethel Merman.
Their huge voices wow Manhattan,
belt tunes so loud
they shake Yankee Stadium
bleachers, box seats, outfield,
vibrate the Bronx
all the way to Yonkers.

Women who dare a microphone
strong enough
to entertain five boroughs,
their music filling every ear.

No measly man
orders such big stars
to tie on an apron,
scrub his crummy floor,
bring him his meatloaf.

Nobody tells Sophie Tucker
to go on a diet, drink fewer
egg creams, cut down
on the caramel.

She belts how a man's
gonna miss her
one who'll learn
it's too late for a chump
who can't appreciate
a woman who will not
keep her mouth shut.

STRUDEL

*Strudel making is not a picnic. So better you should find a nice
bakery and buy your strudel there.*
Ruth and Bob Grossman

Give me a nice rye bread well-browned, a nice piece of strudel, a nice
corned beef or pastrami, a nice tongue. That's not a nice way to talk.
Make nice Jewish friends. Marry a nice Jewish boy. Be nice to me, I
might die soon. Nice and easy. Play nice. That's a nice way to treat
your parents. Nice going. Nice try. Nice as pie. Some nice present you
brought me. If you can't say anything nice, don't say anything. Some
nice mouth you have. Nice and loud. Get a nice job as a teacher with
summers off. Some nice weather we're having. This is the nicest thing
anyone's ever done for me. Nice gesture. Make nice. Be nice to me
I might die soon. Did you forget? Another nice mess you've made.
Nice way to talk to us. Some nice daughter you turned out to be. Nice
sermon. Nice music. Nice eulogy. Nice funeral. So nice of you to come.
So nice of you to invite me. So nice of you to remember. Nice knowing
you. Have a nice day, a nice trip, a nice life. Nice as can be. Nice and
fattening. Nice and juicy. Nice and hot.

THE ONLY LAND SHE EVER OWNED IS HER PLOT AT MOUNT HOPE CEMETERY

My parents never spoke Yiddish with me,
but I picked up insults like *Nem dem*
cup und clap en vant: Take your head
and hit it against the wall. Worse,
Dad would shout into the kitchen
Mom sweating over steaming pots,
chicken fat stink, fans pushing around
gray air. I understand her exasperation
cooking three full meals a day, crammed
into a kitchen so narrow you could reach
the walls arms extended.
She ironed in the bedroom,
my place for sleeping, but not my room,
shoving the iron back and forth,
me not taking a turn, nor asked to.
I gobbled the food, slid down the banister.
Don't, she'd yell, *You'll fall and kill yourself*,
while every second that bomb
of my father's possible relapse hissed,
no vacations in sun for them after radiation
burned his skin, and his required mouth
cleansing routine meant not one meal out
as husband and wife ever. All those years,
when he shouted, *What's for dinner?*
I dreaded her answer, the Yiddish joke:
a shisele drek, a pot of shit.

WONTON SOUP

My face sweats when I realize too late,
after I've ordered the won ton soup
in the Bronx Chinese restaurant: pork
dumplings, in front of Aunt Henny and Nessy.
How could I be so foolish when I don't even like
pig, but the flavorful broth. Of course, they
ordered the meatless sweet and sour.

I know my aunts don't eat meat in non-kosher
restaurants, but pork, lobster, shrimp, crab
are the ultimate taboos. I could have hired
a sound truck to blast the announcement,
Our Oregon niece, the renegade rule flaunter,
doesn't keep kosher.

At least I didn't dig myself deeper, ordering
my favorite shrimp in lobster sauce.
We all spoon our soups and chat gladly
Henny eighty-nine, smart in a red beret and collar,
Nessy in subtle brown, pert wren at seventy-five,
spectacular two-aunt debate team I'd put up against
any politicians.

It's not like the rabbinical council certified
the kitchen, and who's to say the sweet and sour
soup wasn't simmered in a pot where some *traif,*
item boiled before. But American Jews
make allowances for Chinese cuisine.
I've never seen a Jewish neighborhood
without a Chinese eatery.

So nothing happened, I mean, my aunts
never let the conversation flag, hugged
me close when we rose to leave, regardless
of the pork bits stuck in my teeth, my
unkosher kisses on their cheeks.

PEACHES

You're not gonna waste a crop like that,
not with what they charge at the IGA
and factory-canned never tastes flavourful
not after you've enjoyed home-canned.

Pick Fairhavens and Elbertas.
They grow best in this valley.
In the hot, then cold
makes 'em easier to peel.

Feed the peel to the cattle.
They love the snack.
Sometimes I even think I taste
a hint of that sweetness
in the meat.

Let the fruit cool good
and use a real sharp knife
to slice them even.
Quarters pack easier than halves.

Pour in syrup,
tighten the lids,
but not too much,
and be sure to time the boil.

What I love best
is how the kitchen smells fragrant.

Make sure all the screens
on the windows are shut tight
or the butterflies and bees
flit in here to sip the pools
of juice on the counter.
Who can blame them?

The hardest part is lifting
the huge kettle off the stove.
There's no one to call for help
when crops need harvesting
and the men are on the combine
sunup to sundown.

No, I don't can every last peach.
A good batch, a couple of bushels worth,
I cut up raw, sprinkle with preservative
and put in freezer bags for baking.

Tell me now what beats
homemade peach pie, cobbler,
or waffles topped with dollops
of fresh cream, and I'll tell you
nothing in this world tastes better.

SO MUCH SHE SHOULDN'T SAY

Aishes chayel, a woman of valor
like in King Solomon's verse
recited at funerals. She sacrifices
jobs, vacations, when he gets cancer,
can't swallow.

A psychiatrist he waves away
but can't stop tears dripping
on the oxygen line,
IV tethering him to bed.
Never does the husband gain back flesh,
muscle taken from the jaw,
the smooth voice.
The rattle can't be helped.

The rabbi, jolly nosher of Sisterhood blintzes,
repeats pleas of a million rabbis
in prayer shawls with Hebrew letters
embroidered golden on blue velvet,
swaths of silk the Mrs. Rabbis
iron creaseless.

The pious man's words don't
remove surgeries and scars.
Learned in Torah, he echoes Moses
who doesn't mention *his better half.*
Bless her duty, loyalty, unbeatable
gefilte fish, home-baked
chocolate-almond macaroons.

Spoonful by spoonful, pudding,
apple sauce, and chicken soup
she tips gingerly into his mouth.
Live, goddamn you, live.

MY PLOT

Someday I will probably lie
near Floyd in the ground.
The cemetery adjoins
his and Dorothy's house
up Marion Hill Road.
Fifty plus years they
maintained those plots.

One day in his front room
speaking of bargaining, he said,
I jewed them down,
but then turned to me
his nightmare daughter-in-law,
older than his son, divorced,
Jewish New Yorker with a child –
Guess I can't say that any more.

Another visit he said two plots
in the cemetery had come available,
fifty dollars apiece and he'd checked
if an un-embalmed body
in a plain pine box
with a service in Hebrew
could be buried there.

He winked at me,
You're good to go.

AFTER A HARD LIFE

Uncombed, face pillow-smashed,
housecoat over nightie, bunions
squeezed in slippers, she stands
supplicant before flames.

The aluminum percolator
ticks like teletype code
coffee torrents whooshing
through chambered grounds.

Plain Jane tap water transforms
to sultry pleasure. She savors
the fragrant sips that nearly burn,
lights the day's first Lucky

inhales the calm of smoke
cigarette between fingers
a la Marlene Dietrich
blessedly alone.

WONDERS NEVER CEASE

Mother's cooking tasted truly dreadful,
though we'd shovel in huge amounts—
the old Jewish joke: *Such terrible food
and such small portions!*

Kosher beef, the blood drained,
limp French style green beans—
Yonkers haute cuisine a la Birdseye.
We survived on bakery layer cake
and chocolate cream pie.

Later, it amazed me how Mother and Sadie Gluck,
the whole crew of fat women, got swept up
in the Diet Watchers craze, stuck with it,
and Mother, *G-d bless her*, lost sixty pounds.

Konrad Lorenz, hold onto your birdseed.
Women are not geese, after all, imprinted for life.
The holiday goose, cups of *schmaltz*
drained from the greasy meat, disappeared.

There in Yonkers, women
trashed their muumuus, swigged diet cola,
sprinkled Sweet and Low on their grapefruit halves,
outlived their husbands.

IV

UNTOPPLED

September sunlight flames flushed
skin of the Early Girls, the tomatoes
warm in her broad
farm-woman hands.

Spade stuck in the row end dirt,
she works long-handled tools
during the hours she will ignore
her arthritic back.

She bends to pick lemon cucumber,
unstoppable zucchini, everything
ripe in the plot abandoned the terrible
years when Floyd succumbed.

Each step sinks a boot print
amid loaded rows, green stink
of vine, edible leaf and fruit
spicing the sunsets.

Her sunflowers stand erect:
Fiesta del Sol, Italian Whites,
ten foot Bandoliers, Cinnamon Queens
grown from seed.

THE SORROW OF MESHARI AL GHARABALI

Inside his elbow
Meshari holds the drum
inlaid with mother of pearl.

Our class listens.
The voice of the drum
whispers, entices.

The melody is from Kuwait.
The Iraqi War, an everyday
lesson of childhood.

He plays only after
we beg him
and even then

blushes
stammering about
a lack of skill.

The drum
is surprisingly small,
and he sings in Arabic

about a woman
lovely
as a garden.

The drumskin
becomes a moon
white and far away.

PANTOUM FOR DOROTHY AT 92

No longer able to steer her walker,
she's pushed to the table in a wheelchair.
I slice the layer cake I brought her.
After lunch, a Hospice aide will wash her hair.

She's pushed to the table in a wheelchair,
barely manages to lift her spoon.
After lunch, a Hospice aide will wash her hair.
It's gotten hard to bathe her well, alone.

Barely manages to lift her spoon.
I'm happy she can chew soft cake.
It's gotten hard to bathe her well, alone.
When I arrived at 1:00, she was awake.

I'm happy she can chew soft cake
but her eyes look clouded and undone.
When I arrived at 1:00, she was awake.
Her roses framed us when I married her son.

Her eyes look clouded and undone.
She will nap in a recliner, not a bed.
Her roses framed us when I married her son.
She canned cherries every summer and baked bread.

She will nap in a recliner, not a bed
though she's sleeping more and more.
She canned cherries every summer and baked bread,
met Floyd, returned to Portland from the war.

Though she's sleeping more and more,
a fleece Trailblazer blanket keeps her warm.
She met Floyd, returned to Portland from the war.
They raised cattle and three children on this farm.

A fleece Trailblazer blanket keeps her warm.
When I ask how she feels, she says, *Tired.*
They raised cattle and three children on this farm.
It's been over seven years since Floyd died.

When I ask how she feels. She says, *Tired.*
Does she mean "of living" or she wants to rest?
It's been over seven years since Floyd died.
There's so much a stoic farmwife won't express.

Does she mean "of living" or she wants to rest?
After lunch, a Hospice aide will wash her hair.
There's so much a stoic farmwife won't express
pushed from the table in a wheelchair.

ADIÓS, ROBERTO

Wild cucumber
bursts out of nowhere
twisting
wide leaves
darken the buds

Whoever thinks nature
is gentle
has not watched
blackberry conquer

Oregon
without pickers
overripe cherries
strawberries rot

My student Roberto
whispers *Salvador*
asylum denied

He pays a fee
Gonif
my father's word
for lawyer
means devil

Roberto writes me letters
to practice English

I who have never
had to work
the fields

AUTUMN RETREAT ON THE BREITENBUSH RIVER

Sun deceives this October
afternoon of record lows.

The red-breasted sapsucker
drills the Douglas fir trunk,

makes balancing sideways
look so easy.

The cabin is icy, the table, the beds.
I stoke cedar for the quick burn,

fiddle with propane heater controls,
smell gas. This could all explode:

a spark, whosh,
disfigurement for life.

Lit tongues of kerosene lamps
smear shadows across murky walls.

Even under down quilts
my face aches.

I wonder if my husband,
at home, can sleep. We guess

he'll keep his job, but what about
those with less seniority?

I startle awake, a woodpecker's
work. Overnight, the fire's died.

Frozen ground cracks
where ice stabs through.

CINCO DE MAYO

The rhododendron exhausts
itself with blooming.
A cat sleeps under
the front bumper.
May lawn daisies lose
their heads to the mower,
but peonies that disappointed
last year promise heavy flowering.

The Olympic torch
arrives at the capitol
as the Sprague Olympian
Marching Band belts out
a rousing "Chariots of Fire."
Smug blackberry prepares again
to dominate. *This is not
a holiday we celebrate
in my country*, José insists.

The faucet leaks all night.
Mossy lichen spreads
up the trunk and branches.
Madonna is big with child,
but she won't name him Jesus.
Lilacs begin to brown.
In the E.S.L. student movie
the groom is hauled away
by immigration.

The latest memo said
classrooms are sacrosanct.
If immigration officers come,
send them to security.
Teach students to say, *I'd like
my lawyer present.*

OY, YONKERS

The one crime I knew
was Mother snitching grapes
at Smilen's Fruit Store
Go ahead, she'd whisper,
everybody does it.

This visit, outside
Mother's building
a woman with a baby
in a car seat slows,
extends her hand
for the bag of white powder.

I'm told not to walk –
even in the daytime –
on Carol Avenue
where Rachel Goldberg
lived up the marble staircase

in the six room apartment
where we devoured entire boxes
of Girl Scout mint cookies,
the sunken living room
big as a swimming pool.

The Parkhill Theater,
where *Gigi* and *My Fair Lady*
thrilled us, is now
La Iglesia de La Virgen,
and a sidewalk drunk stabs
dollar bills toward mother's face.

She, who in her right mind
would be the first
to flee him,
won't budge.

Nobody in our building
moved away:
On the sidewalk,
my mother, Francis Glick,
Martha Lesh, Ellie Adler,
sat daily in their folding chairs,
so what move
could *I* make without
somebody's mother knowing?

DEPARTMENT OF LABOR SENIOR INVESTIGATOR

He brings home heaps of handbags,
transistor radios, bakery goods—
you name it from his job.

I want to excuse him as kind-hearted,
but sometimes phoning from home
he warns bosses of investigations.

I want to say in his defense
that he dropped out of high school,
delivered telegrams by bicycle,
that his father's business collapsed.

I want you to know he's kind to women,
that he drove Mrs. Kaminetsky
all the way to Long Island
to visit her son in the hospital.

I want to excuse myself,
girl in a white eyelet dress,
teenager in a pink leather jacket
eager for the perfumes he brings me.

What good does it do at twenty
when I refuse to take more,
ask him to stop
and he yells, calls me a fool,

and I stay away
until I'm twenty-two,
what good, now my father's fifty-four
and dead.

MOVING HER

I found Norwegian
cloisonné butterflies,
an ivory chrysanthemum,
diamonds and jade.

Take them with you,
she said. *I won't ever
use them again.
I'm going crazy.*

She wept in the dust
of the nicotine-stained
Bronx apartment,
étagère, chandelier,
gold velvet upholstery,
in the style, a friend of mine
who supervised the movers,
dubbed *Bronx European.*

Everything wrapped for
the three thousand dollar relocation,
the crates I unpacked for her in Oregon.

Looking at those boxes from New York
the after-Dad-had-died new
furniture she'd indulged in,
she mused, *Where
did this come from?
Whose is it?*

Staring at a crystal necklace
as if it were shrouded in clouds,
she wondered,
What is this?

RIVER WE ARE WARNED AGAINST BEFORE WE EVER COME HERE

Walking North Bank Road, Phyllis tells me:
her cousin, the only female Holocaust survivor
from her family stopped by a cafe door with a big
hand suddenly above her head. The S.S. man said,
You don't like me, do you?

We pause on the McKenzie Bridge. While the river
rages under us, she tells me her cousin's brother
wrapped an old lady in a blanket, pushed her out
a train to Auschwitz, and followed, saving
them both. Though the Nazis ransacked their house
in France, she held a yellow cloth star in her hand,
photos of the whole family.

The river is so loud, no one would hear cries
for help from us. After the Allies discovered
death camps, they didn't bomb the tracks.

Phyllis and I have developed a habit, quizzing
each other on the meanings of Yiddish words
we remember. *Punim* for face, *keppeleh* for little head.
What if the S.S. officer had brought his hand down,
crushing her cousin's skull?
He could have done it in one movement, one
push into a current so swift and so chilling.

THE FEEDER TABLE

Mother's face
that crushed flower
droops toward formica.
I natter on about weather
the cold summer
how blooms last longer
though she doesn't answer.

Trays clatter, utensils and plates crash:
time for staff to take their places
inside the horseshoe table
to cajole and shove in mushy blobs.
Green must be beans.
Brown looks like dog shit.

Once Father brought a puppy home,
and Mother said choose her or it.
I wanted the pup.

This week's news reported
an Alzheimer's patient
abandoned at a dog track.

I placed my mother in a *facility*
what she'd call *A fate*
you wouldn't wish on a dog
if she could speak.

One o'clock,
one forty-five,
it's hard to believe a human
could take such tiny bites.
A chihuahua eats more.

NONPAREIL

Would you like a balsamic reduction
on your salmon? The waitress asks.
I'll certainly have to tell this
to Aunt Henny.

It sounds so hoity-toity
we'll laugh that *reduction*
in sauce means inflation in price.

The salmon piece smaller
than my palm
was delicious,
but left me hungry.

Leave Henny's hungry?
Never. How could I?
My last visit to Yonkers,
she baked chocolate mandelbrot,
and noodle kugel with cinnamon,
golden raisins and sour cream.

Ignoring her arthritis,
congestive heart,
she popped in a cassette
of *Fascination,*
said, *I'll lead.*
She waltzed us
around her kitchen,
bum feet and all.

I'll call her on the weekend
when it's free, tell her
she packed her thumb-print cookies
so well, not one white-dotted
nonpareil fell off.

OLD AGE ALPHABET

A is Alzheimer's,
Ronald Reagan lending it
a certain celebrity.

B for behavior
badly out of whack,

and *C* is the Camels
chain-smoked.

D denotes dementia.

E is extra care, extra cost.

F, of course, for the *f* word,
family, fiasco.

Gee, gotta go.

H is Hell—
I sure hope
this isn't hereditary.

J must be Job.
Why God, why?

K is *kvetch.*
Did you forget you had a mother?

L for *latkes*
that used to sizzle.

M for Mama,
those syllables that bleat.

N is for nursing home,
nauseous, and nobody's fault.

O is *oy* and *Out, out—*

P is for *potchkeh* as in
her in the kitchen
potchkehing around.

Q is the quiet in disquiet.

R is for a room reeking
Pinesol and urine.

S hisses *shmatte*, like that old
housedress she cleaned in.

T tsedrater kup, deranged head:
stuffing silverware in her purse.

U, useful or useless, used up.
What's the use?

V is pet visits,
her arthritic hand
stroking the dog's fur.

W is wishing for one lucid
moment, that I'd been
kinder when she was well.

X is for xylophone
notes of one simple song
after another.

Y is *Yes,*
we have no bananas,
we crooned together.

Z is zilch, taking
motion, function, breath
and zero remains.

MOTHER WAS LEAVING EARTH

leaving Santiam Unit room 302,
Sublimity, Oregon,
the bariatric non-pressure mattress
and bedsore bandages,
the chart listing who turned her
in her nightgown and diaper.

My mother was leaving
and my doctor who'd gone
with me to the nursing home
a day earlier,
because I'd told her
I was worried
said, *She knows it's you.*
She wants to go,
give her permission.

But even so,
when the phone rang
in my house that April
lilacs blooming heedlessly,
it was not my mother
calling to wish me *Happy Birthday.*
Did her body know?

The voice was saying
Your mother's stopped
and started breathing.
     Should I come now?
Yes, the nurse said, *Yes.*

My mother didn't go
until I got there,
held her hand,
said, *Thank you, Mama,*
thank you. Go
when you're ready.

Then only I
was breathing
beside the sheets
and patient gown,
the hand cooling.

And only after
could I say,
Don't go,
don't ever go.

LATKE PAGE STAINED BROWN IN MOM'S
SETTLEMENT HOUSE COOKBOOK

She said, *Bubbeleh*, *eat your latkes now, nice
and warm. Don't let them get cold.*

Why, I asked, *do raw potatoes turn black in the bowl?*
They looked like something gulped in the Camps.

*Some questions I can't answer.
Do I look like a scientist?*

The grater nicked her fingers, left
a little blood.

She stood between the sink and stove, the rack
of hand-washed garments hanging above, dripping.

I didn't ask, Would you have left Daddy
if he hadn't had cancer?

Would you have married
if you weren't thirty?

Mom, did you have a favorite song? As I played "I'll
Be Seeing You," you breathed your last.

Was that the right guess?
Did you want silence?

You prayed over the candles, but you never went
to Hebrew school. How did you memorize the words?

You ground apple chunks in the food mill so Daddy
wouldn't choke on your applesauce.

You stood in your housedress, girdle pressing into
thighs. Stockings, tight casings around heavy legs.

The chiropodist plastered bandages on corns that must
have ached, but you never complained to me. Why not?

Watch, or they'll burn. See how nicely they brown?
More sour cream?

You stood turning over pancakes, oil bubbling.
How often did it sting?

OPEN MIC READING OF EROTIC POETRY

Already April, grass gone
lush and tangly.

Plums blossom unabashed
in Portland.

Books call us
menopausal.

My mother used to say,
Good riddance to bad rubbish:

Tampax, diaphragms,
contraceptive gel

and worrying if the blood
seeped through.

At Catbird Seat Bookstore,
the actual bird disturbs the reading.

Cage covered, the bird thinks
night's here, stops squawking.

Not us, women over sixty,
reading our poetry.

AURELIA AURITA: MOON JELLY

No one cares about undress in the sea
Milky pink lingerie can't camouflage
my stomachs and radial canals
Aren't we all
water-filled
animals

Diaphanous parachute transparent moon
I contract
and expand
contract
and expand
no heart
spine
eye
ear
nor anxious brain

Muscle pulsation flings
plankton shrimp mollusks
against
my mucal skin

I sway delicate flagellate solicitation
but
don't think
you can grab
or
fondle me

Call me *Medusa Saucer Umbrella*
Silk Camisole
Belle

I lurk below your ocean's shallow rim
No spearless Lolita
venomous
I sting

HIDE-A-BED

How did you manage it, Mom, every
morning folding up twin beds into
the Castro Convertible sectional sofa,
transforming the not-really-a-bedroom
where you and Dad slept, back into
our living room then every night,
hoisting the folded framework
and mattresses out, retrieving pillows
and bedding to spread and tuck in?

How many times did we glare
at those TV advertisements playing
the chipper, ding-a-ling melody behind
the slogan: *Buy a Castro Convertible sofa*
as a night-gowned girl skipped and flicked
the couch open into a bed, one-handed?

You bent double till your back ached,
stretched arms from shoulders scarred
by bursitis surgery, curved fingers growing stiff
and thick from years of gripping
metal rods, yanking them up, slamming
beds down. Your daughter slept
like other children in a normal bed.

Mom, after just three nights
at a seaside motel, having wrestled
the hide-a-bed in and out, attempting
to sleep on the ridges of a thin mattress,
no comfortable position possible
on the rude metal bars, I swear never
to make this mistake again.

On the multi-thousand dollar Bariatric
Alternating Pressure Mattress Medicare
finally provided to reduce the stress
on bedsores that never healed, you lay,
leg bent, and no way, short of breaking bones,
could you unfold.

PURPLE QUESTIONS

The bruise purples, my thigh aches.
How in the world did you do that?
I don't know any more than how
damp irises bleed purple puddles
or our lilac bush, toppled in winter,
perfumes the April air.

Why call Manishewitz *red*
with its purple hue, praise
as *purple mountains majesty*,
granite marbled gray and white.

Purple People Eater, one-eyed
and hungry. What makes a nutty
song like that a hit? And why do
bouquets of violets look so tender?

What pheromones connect us,
so no matter how dark the bruise,
the mark fades, pain disappears,
and though your lips no longer
kiss me there, the memory stays?

PRAISE

Praise the night nurse
who changes diapers
on old men and women,
who bathes them tenderly
brushes their hair
smoothes bedclothes
lifts their glasses of water.

Praise the day nurse
lifting the spoon
removing bandages
applying salve
wrapping the sores.

Praise the headnurse
who in all honesty indicates
which doctor not to listen to
which treatments make sense
in her long experience.

Praise the doctor
who offers to visit
confirms a need for morphine
advises giving
permission to go
promises it will be soon.

Praise the husband
who drives that final evening
who sits beside his wife
holding her hand as they watch
the funeral employee
wheeling the body to the unmarked van,

and friends, family
who bring casseroles, geraniums,
who write words of comfort,
hold the grieving in their arms,

and last but not least
praise death,
that one breath not taken,
Death who did the job
and got out.

MANHATTAN *MATZO BREI*

a delicacy in 2014 on the summer bill of fare
at Russ and Daughters Café on the Lower Eastside—
once a tumult of refugees in teeming tenements
chewing this old country mish-mosh—
listed now beside paddlefish caviar,
a hundred bucks plus, under beet and lemon
shrub—an icy American colonial aperitif
of vinegar-dashed fruit.

I'd be *mishugeh*, a total nutcase,
to imply my parents imbibed
any such drink on Passover at seders
instead of strictly kosher Manischewitz.
Mama and I woke before Papa to break
the matzos, dropped pieces into a bowl of milk
and let them soak, softened, no sharp edges
left to scrape the linings of our mouths.

We sprinkled in salt from the shaker used
to add the Seder plate's tears. This modern
matzo brei's thin as a shingle. And sorry,
but an apple sauce side goes with latkes,
not Passover breakfast. How do we stomach
anything in New York humidity, or did we
back on nights when we recited the plagues—

lice, vermin, murder of the enemy's first born?
It became game-like, dipping fingertips into wine,
tapping drops on our plates to signify blood.
I recited: *Ma nishtanah halilah hazeh mikol haleitlot?*
"Why is this night different from all other nights?"
but questioned nothing, fork jabbed into the brisket,
matzo meal cake, and macaroons. Mornings
I gobbled my plate heaped full of matzo brei.

Today on my I-Phone news, fleeing
refugees grasp bundles of bread, rice, water,
family if they're lucky. I await my bill
in air-conditioning at a marble table, jars of
kosher pickles lining shelves as decoration.
Matzo brei eaten, glad it's on somebody's menu,
I long to savor the bread of affliction reformed—
oval-shaped, golden-colored, soft.

BEACH PEAS

Here they go again,
insinuating themselves
across rocks the size
of toddler's fists,
scrambling at the estuary's edge.
Noon's tidal pool
drags the Salmon River
inland and wind snarls
hair against my face.

Purple flower clusters
puffed cheerleader perky,
innocent as Amish bonnets.
Oval leaflets in pairs slap
veined surfaces
or applaud those gulls
able to balance on stones.

EPITHALAMION (27 YEARS LATER)

after Stephanie Lenox

My husband sweeps pine needles off the roof.
Matted oak leaves no longer block the skylight.
A rag swirls in his hand, small for a man.

God forbid any father in my childhood should take that
cockamamie kind of chance, balancing on a steep slant
where you can slip one-two-three and break your neck.

Forget seeing Dad in jeans or work boots on our flat
tar roof. If it needed cleaning, our building super Louie
would take care of that.

Through the curved glass now, Kevin mouths, "Better?"
Sky surrounds him in powder blue. Not a *mishugena*
nutcase cowboy, the way we labeled the guys in Nowhereland

past New York, above California. But my husband isn't any
Galloping, *Hi-Yo, Silver* Lone Ranger. He lowers his broom
through the attic window, climbs inside. Home safe.

Years ago, a storm knocked down our cherry tree, roots half-
exposed. *It's alive* he said. *Let's leave it.* I pestered him to chop
the remains. But today, a decade later, the limbs are trunks.

He taught me to call the black-crested, azure bird landing
on our tidy roof with fruit in its beak a Steller's jay,
explained the airborne mews, chirps and barks.

Jays mimic other birds and animals. *That's a robin's cry.*
In Yonkers, sure, I recognized robins, but who bothered
to listen long enough to memorize their song?

Cherries stain our lips. I brush needles from his hair.
Have we had a hug today? he asks. In his arms, I inhale
fir, cherry and oak, Oregon. *Oy*, such a fragrance.

CORDATE SHAPE

The stone resembles a valentine
but smooth, calcified and white.
It will never become a human heart,
require surgery, digitalis or aspirin,
emergency resuscitation. It may consider
life lucky no matter how much
ocean and rivers batter and bash.
It will not await biopsy reports, scans,
blood test results by telephone or mail,
won't be shown color photos, be told
or left to deduce that suspicious lines
may disappear, be nothing, prove fatal.
No bucket-list wish to grant returns
a stone to shore. It will not moan or sob
or gasp or hack or shriek. A hand pockets
it to take home as a cheerful souvenir.
One splash of incoming tide, that's that.
Its indentation disappears from sand.

Lois Rosen retired from a career of teaching English as a Second Language at Chemeketa Community College in Salem, Oregon. She's taught in Colombia, Japan, and Ecuador. At Willamette University, she co-directed the Advanced Institute of the Oregon Writing Project, taught Creative Writing as a Visiting Assistant Professor, and leads writing groups for the Institute for Continued Learning. The Oregon Teachers as Writers Contest, The James de Priest Contest of the Oregon Symphony at Western Oregon University, the Oregon State Poetry Association, and the Oregon Writers' Colony have awarded her poetry prizes. Her poems and stories have appeared in over a hundred journals including most recently: *Calyx Journal, The Jewish Women's Literary Annual, VoiceCatcher, Alimentum: the Literature of Food,* and *The Night, and the Rain, and the River.* Traprock Books published her first poetry book, *Pigeons,* in 2004. The Rainier Writing Workshop granted her an MFA in Fiction and a Debra Tall Memorial Scholarship in 2010. Centrum published her short fiction chapbook, *Layer Cake*, in 2014.

Particular thanks to my husband, Kevin Davidson, my son and daughter-in-law, David and Bree Rosen, Slavey Tolev and Meredith Martin, dear family, my steadfast friends, and the editors who have published my work. Gratitude goes to all my teachers, students, and fellow writers including those from the Oregon Writing Project at Willamette University, The Centrum Writers' Conference, PDX Writers, The Squaw Valley Community of Writers, Flight of the Mind, the Trillium Writers, the ICL Writers, the 9th Street Writers, and the ESL Department at Chemeketa Community College. Deep appreciation to Centrum, Vermont Studio Center, the Anderson Center, Soapstone, and the Oregon Writers Colony for residencies. Eleanor Berry, Virginia Corrie-Cozart, Marilyn Johnston, Stephanie Lenox, Ada Molinoff, Colette Tennant, and Dina Triest—The Peregrine Poets of Salem, Oregon—have been a huge boon to my writing and my life. Special thanks, too, to poets: CaroleAnn Crateau, April Ossman, Paulann Petersen, Toni Hanner, Carolyn Miller, Erik Muller, Willa Schneberg, Cindy Williams Gutierrez, and Chris Howell. With appreciation to Susan Trueblood Stuart for the cover art, Susan Lee Graves for the author photo, my publisher, Mifanwy Kaiser, and all the skilled, big-hearted people at Tebot Bach, who strengthen community through poetry.

TEBOT BACH
A 501(c) (3) Literary Arts Education Non Profit

THE TEBOT BACH MISSION: advancing literacy, strengthening community, and transforming life experience with the power of poetry through readings, workshops, and publications.

THE TEBOT BACH PROGRAMS

1. A poetry reading and writing workshop series for venues such as homeless shelters, battered women's shelters, nursing homes, senior citizen daycare centers, Veterans organizations, hospitals, AIDS hospices, correctional facilities which serve under-represented populations. Participating poets include: John Balaban, Brendan Constantine, Megan Doherty, Richard Jones, Dorianne Laux, M.L. Leibler, Lawrence Lieberman, Carine Topal, Cecilia Woloch.

2. A poetry reading and writing workshop series for the Southern California community at large, and for schools K-University. The workshops feature local, national, and international teaching poets. Participating poets have include: David St. John, Charles Webb, the late Wanda Coleman, Amy Gerstler, Patricia Smith, Holly Prado, Dorothy Barresi, W.D. Ehrhart, Tom Lux, Rebecca Seiferle, Suzanne Lummis, Michael Datcher, B.H. Fairchild, Cecilia Woloch, Chris Abani, Laurel Ann Bogen, Sam Hamill, David Lehman, Christopher Buckley, & Mark Doty.

3. A publishing component to give local, national, and international poets a venue for publishing and distribution.

Tebot Bach
Box 7887
Huntington Beach, CA 92615-7887
714-968-0905
www.tebotbach.org